"Layered, complex, and infinitely compelling, Chet'la Sebree's *Field Study* is a daring exploration of the self and our interactions with others— a meditation on desire, race, loss, and survival. In this moment of American reckoning, Sebree shows us—intimately and with vulnerability— the truth of our shared history: that 'even when we aren't talking about race we are.'"

—Natasha Trethewey, author of *Memorial Drive*

"Woven from the rough threads of race, legacy, and love, *Field Study* is a groundbreaking book that vibrates with truth and lyrical beauty. A profound poetic talent, Chet'la Sebree has created a brilliant book that both haunts and heals."

—Ada Limón, author of *The Carrying*

"Chet'la Sebree's *Field Study* is a long look at those aspects of a self that are often most difficult to look at—chiefly, the woundedness from which we make our loves, and the wounding loves we both flee and mourn. In prose poetry that at crucial moments brilliantly enacts via its syntax the poet's struggle to look away from that which she must record, Sebree has composed an elegy that is, especially in its music, as alive as a celebration."

—Shane McCrae, author of *Sometimes I Never Suffered*

"With its steady capture of memory recalled, quotes, moments from real and represented (fictive) life, Chet'la Sebree's *Field Study* assembles an exquisite and propulsive leap into the aftermath of a relationship with a white man— only to land with the grace of a skilled dancer. Elliptically reminiscent of Lily Hoang's *A Bestiary* and Sarah Manguso's *Ongoingness*, this is not an autoethnography by a Black woman, but an immaculate bricolage that both confronts and reckons various channels of knowing and being with the messy, complicated desires of inter- and intraracial relationships. Here is a woman who does not 'avoid speaking a violence.' Of a wound in healing, Sebree writes that she 'pick[s] until no remnants of a scab exist'; in peering deeply into the crevasses of pop culture, critical race studies, and literature, she clears the surface not for restoration, but for unhindered transcendence."

—Diana Khoi Nguyen, author of *Ghost Of*

"Chet'la Sebree's *Field Study* is a luminous, multi-layered treatise on the complexities of race and desire in America. In contemplating the aftermath of an interracial relationship, the work virtuosically entwines memory with history, literature, pop culture, and critical theory. This is a wise, generous work that holds out hope for all kinds of grace, even as it acknowledges the aches and perils of our current polarized moment."

—Kiki Petrosino, author of *White Blood: A Lyric of Virginia*

75
FSG

Shannon Woodloe

Chet'la Sebree
Field Study

CHET'LA SEBREE is the director of the Stadler
Center for Poetry and Literary Arts at Bucknell
University and the author of *Mistress*, which won
the 2018 New Issues Poetry Prize and was nomi-
nated for a 2020 NAACP Image Award. She earned
an MFA in creative writing, with a focus in poetry,
from American University and has received fellow-
ships from the Delaware Division of the Arts,
MacDowell, Hedgebrook, Yaddo, the Vermont
Studio Center, and the Robert H. Smith Inter-
national Center for Jefferson Studies. Her poetry
has appeared in the *Kenyon Review*, *Guernica*,
Pleiades, and other publications.

ALSO BY CHET'LA SEBREE

Mistress

Field	Study

| Field | Study |

Chet'la Sebree

FSG Originals

Farrar, Straus and Giroux

New York

FSG Originals
Farrar, Straus and Giroux
120 Broadway, New York 10271

Library of Congress Cataloging-in-Publication Data
Names: Sebree, Chet'la, author.
Title: Field study / Chet'la Sebree.
Description: First edition. | New York : FSG Originals / Farrar,
    Straus and Giroux, 2021.
Identifiers: LCCN 2020058348 | ISBN 9780374539023
    (trade paperback)
Subjects: LCGFT: Poetry.
Classification: LCC PS3619.E275 F54 2021 | DDC 811/.6—dc23
LC record available at https://lccn.loc.gov/2020058348

Designed by Gretchen Achilles

Our books may be purchased in bulk for promotional,
educational, or business use. Please contact your local
bookseller or the Macmillan Corporate and Premium Sales
Department at 1-800-221-7945, extension 5442, or by email
at MacmillanSpecialMarkets@macmillan.com.

www.fsgoriginals.com • www.fsgbooks.com
Follow us on Twitter, Facebook, and Instagram at @fsgoriginals

10 9 8 7 6 5 4 3 2 1

for those seeking whole
with the holes they see

Black women do not have all the answers. We are not superheroes, and ours is not the definite worldview. But we are trustworthy subjects, of our own experiences and of ways of knowing.

—TRESSIE McMILLAN COTTOM

Field	Study

I'm not good at small talk.

———

At a former colleague's dinner party, I was talking about life, about desire, about this and how I've basically been single for five years.

This feels like an overshare—now and then.

Someone tells me this is the beginning.

———

Field research is the collection of observational information. Approaches vary across disciplines.

This field is my brain's backlog of books and a lot of bedrooms.

This field has maps made of men, of finger pads, of scrotal sacs. My muscles a Moleskine.

3.

Analysis: trapped between my split nails, their skin cells.

———

Or was the beginning the basement of a church converted into a place of poetry worship with coffee and chocolate and another Black woman?

I thought maybe I'd start with the night I met you—a scene that unfolded around a dining room table.

———

I didn't think I'd start with two men—one white, one Black—at a dinner party.

I knew and didn't know these men had life-altering things happening—illness, retirement, death in the family. These all feel more important than this and their races, but sadly those won't be the stories I'm telling.

———

After you moved across the country, leaving me in our city, a white friend asked me why I'd dated you, a white man.

4.

I said something about your hazel eyes and thick brown hair.

At last suggested, it could have something to do with the past.

———

Fetish: a sexual desire in which gratification is linked to fixation.

———

Were white men my kink?

———

At the Bedford Reformatory for Women, same-sex interracial relationships were referred to as "harmful intimacies."

———

An anthropological field study makes it easier to breathe when my heart aches at the sight of ambering leaves.

———

5.

Someone asked if I was writing an auto-ethnography in poetry.

A character study, a fiction, a script.

———

In the belly of the building, the Black woman asked, *Do you still watch* Scandal*?*

———

When we look at the screen all we see is ourselves . . . all you can do is comment on whether you feel it is a good resemblance or not . . . This is a conscious, clearly ego-directed, activity.

—MIKE KELLEY

———

But what if you're an infant first admiring your reflection, reaching out to see if those soft-fleshed hands reach back?

———

When my father tells me I'm beautiful, I cross my eyes and curl the corner of my upper lip.

———

Let me begin by saying my father is not perfect, that my mother may think I need to learn this.

———

As a child, I wondered why all my white classmates had hair that cascaded like cartoon characters'.

———

Disappointed that @GraziaUK edited out & smoothed my hair to fit a more Eurocentric notion of what beautiful looks like.

—LUPITA NYONG'O

———

I fear this tweet will go the way of MySpace and AIM, but that the sentiment will remain the same.

————

My father hopes I'll let people see the me he sees before I curl my lip.

————

Twenty years since my hair has lapped the creamy crack, my hair stays straight with more ease after trees lose their leaves.

————

To be clear, here, I won't bear the weight of white legibility.

————

My great-grandmother was paper-bag-test-passing high yellow.

My grandmother has always been particular about pigmentation, was the first to protest my "natural naps."

She called out *Grandson* when she first met you.

8. It was 2011.

We're still stuck in the Doll Test.

———

Note: I ask a few Black friends if they consider me light-skin.

One: [*laughs hysterically*]

Another: *depends on who you're asking.*

———

Teach her to cook, my great-gran said to my mom of me. *She's too pretty to be in the kitchen, but teach her anyway.*

———

Inception: the establishment or starting point of an institution or activity.

———

Whiteness is such the American default that it has even colonized our imaginations.

—DAMON YOUNG

———

Perhaps I was Pecola seeking the bluest eye in another.

———

When I was a child, none of the kissing scenes featured men with my coloring.

The closest: Aladdin, my favorite.

———

In *Inception*, dreams are used to implant an idea into someone's subconscious.

In my dreams, white men have figured prominently.

In my dreams, after these years, you're still one of them.

———

In his dissertation, Ross Gay states "this study . . . blends my love of literature with my desire to understand my own subject position and my own family history in relation to

American's historical preoccupation with interracial desire." It prompts my own investigation.

I find interesting the covers of some topical tomes: two-tone, ice-cream cone; a Black woman presented as dead-eyed doe.

Another's title fashioned after a familiar familial adage: *don't bring a white boy home.*

———

I guess the beginning would be preschool and a boy named Connor.

Or maybe I'm older.

Maybe it starts with Bobby or Eric or Dan or Dan or you or Dan again.

What can I say?

I was born in the eighties, went to a lot of white schools. Dan was a popular white boy name.

I was one of the few Black girls in class. One of the ones with a name that didn't pass.

———

*I am the only Negro in the United States
whose grandfather on the mother's side was
not an Indian chief.*

—ZORA NEALE HURSTON

———

Unlike Hurston's, my family lore supported
the national Negro story. That's why great-
gran was so light, had "good hair"—silver
strands that used to slip through the teeth of
silver hair-comb clips.

23andMe has shown me that my family
constructed these stories for the sake of
sanity.

These narratives persist.

Sometimes we avoid speaking a violence.

———

Hagar is asked to lend her body to whatever
cause it suits.

———

In a crowded Thai restaurant, in a small town, in the center of a state, a visiting speaker implied that I was a slave to my colleague, a white man.

This was after he said *Damn! That's Black!* about my name.

He was a Black man.

———

Note: It feels complicated to note this.

It feels like a betrayal, a disservice.

———

Black women and girls face additional burdens of protecting the reputations of black boys and men.

—TRESSIE McMILLAN COTTOM

———

My brother and dad drove nine hours through a snowstorm to get to me.

My grandfather prayed with my mother daily.

I don't know if I'll know their levels of love romantically.

————

Men make bad decisions.

So do women.

We have to forge forward with what we are given.

————

Intraracially . . . [straight black men's] relationship to and with black women is not unlike whiteness's relationship to us.

—DAMON YOUNG

————

In a classroom experiment, bell hooks asked her students in *which racialized body would they choose* to be reincarnated.

Rarely did even Black women choose themselves.

———

The Women's March meant a lot to a lot of women in my life.

By a lot of women in my life, I mean the 53% of my friends that are white.

With them, I don't have to differentiate between "women" and "white women" because when I say "women," at least 53% of the time people—and by "people," I mean "white people"—will assume I mean "white women."

These percentages are as fake as fake news but this fact is not: white people see whiteness as universal.

There is no appropriate antonym for those of us who are not.

———

To say this . . . is great because it transcends its
particularity to say something "human" . . . is
to reveal . . . the stance that people of color
are not human, only achieve the human in
certain circumstances.

—CLAUDIA RANKINE and BETH LOFFREDA

———

If I erase part of myself to make another part
whole, I still end up only half a self.

I've never been good at math but that doesn't
add up, so I don't march.

———

Our pussies do not unite us.

—MORGAN JERKINS

———

I grew up feeling like the mealworm in flour
or the pearl in an oyster bushel—a nuisance
or a token to be pocketed, coveted, shown, as
if my opalescence was a shelter against my
classmates' racism.

16.

Swimming in an oft milk-frothed ocean, I picked up a penchant for upticked speech and using *like* like verbal somnambulance.

———

Perhaps the beginning was a door opening.

———

In the forties, Black girls thought Black dolls were ugly.

Same thing happened in the early aughts.

To love ourselves, are we ever truly taught?

———

In 1963, Black women marched separately, had to fight to speak.

DeCuir not as household as *Plessy*.

———

We : still Hagar.

17.

———

Note: These are trail markers.

———

No one . . . has any desire to reckon with the weight of where we've been, which means that no one . . . wants to be free.

—KIESE LAYMON

———

The bull sign I was born under has made me stubborn.

I pick and pick and pick until no remnants of a scab exist.

———

A dance teacher told my mother I didn't have the right body—a child in beginners' ballet.

An early display of pigheadedness: I excelled, skipped intermediate, went straight to advanced.

When commended by the teacher, I quit, never again to do that type of dance.

———

There's a pain that leads to more pain, and there's the pain that leads to freedom.

—REV. ANGEL KYODO WILLIAMS

———

This, for fuck's sake, better be the latter.

———

I am just one woman working toward climax.

———

Sometimes I think I want babies with more manageable hair.

Childhood trauma from periwinkle popcorn tin of balls and barrettes—a recurrent mother-daughter nightmare.

———

Politics of respectability (or, respectability
politics): assimilation, concession to the
mainstream, policing that supports "standard"
American English.

———

Is my fight against the mad Black woman in
me a function of said respectability?

———

Everyone hates a Black woman.

It's hyperbolic.

But it isn't.

———

*Women of Color in america have grown up
within a symphony of anger, at being silenced,
at being unchosen, at knowing that when we
survive, it is in spite of a world that . . . hates
our very existence outside of its service.*

—AUDRE LORDE

———

I have sat at a lot of different tables, have learned that I'm pretty code-switch enabled.

———

In a bar, in a white-liberal-loving city, a white woman moved my body to position hers against a railing.

I am too tall to stand center, she whispered— making me small.

In the same city, in the same week, a white woman spat wine on me.

I was choking, she barked without apology.

To me, these aren't microscopies.

———

I've felt like society's eraser shards—bits used to fix other people's shit, then discarded.

Somehow still a wet nurse from actual babes to Alabama-special-election saves.

———

My secret . . . I'm always angry.

—BRUCE BANNER

———

And why wouldn't I be?

———

My friends call me Captain Save-a-Hoe, but here I'm not trying to save anyone.

Except, maybe, me.

———

Daughter of a hot comb, I oscillate between flat and fro. This prompts people's opinions.

Straight assimilant; curls political.

No reality of versatility.

Everything a statement.

The same extends to the penis I frequent.

———

Stylists have said my hair's kinda coarse.

My contralto is easily hoarse.

My small pear shape has thigh riding high—
it looks like my ass, it reaches around the
side.

In these things, I take pride.

And in August, I risk burn to augment myself
a sweeter color.

———

I've wondered about being too tart, if I'd be a
disappointment to some of my ancestors.

———

When the field's a bar, I take note of what I've
chosen to wear, of my style of hair.

You met me when my hair was straight, bob-
clipped.

The last time we kissed, I was rocking two-
strand twists.

———

When the field's a bed, most men don't give a damn about respectability.

I know porno when I feel one: pump-pump-flip.

When the field's a bed, I care about the girth of his finger, not what color it is.

———

I want to be palm raw and hip-bone sore.

I want it on the bed, on the floor, in the back of my '02 Honda Accord.

I want his fingertips to smooth over me slowly—fingerprint and follicle in holy union.

———

I remember the serrated edge of breath and jut of jaw, when I heavy-panted over your fresh-licked earlobe.

———

I shouldn't say these things; this I know.

I was raised by good, churchgoing people.

———

In the context of American slavery antebellum southerners accepted the image of the sexually insatiable enslaved woman, thereby characterizing all white men as victims of sepia temptresses.

—CHERYL D. HICKS

———

I can see why I should distance myself from this legacy.

Note: Even in this retelling of history, the women are light-skinned.

———

I worry my family will be embarrassed for—and, or, of—me.

That they'll be ashamed of what I'm saying.

But I fear silence like crustacean-crushing mandibles of the deep.

———

[Black women] . . . fashioned a protective silence . . . so successfully that black women eventually "lost the ability to articulate any conception of their sexuality."

—CHERYL D. HICKS

———

I'm not sure if monsters are born or made.

I refuse to be made monster of circumstances.

———

I want to do things differently: night-blooming jasmine, downward-facing trumpet of a tiger lily.

———

I mean, nothing makes me feel more powerful
than when a white dude eats my pussy.

—ALI WONG

———

You called it a *car accident* when my thighs
collapsed together in pleasure.

Was I the most beautiful wreck you'd ever
been in?

———

What do you call
that space between
the dark geographies of sex?

—NATASHA TRETHEWEY

———

With a white man, I worry if I will be seen
as Hottentot Venus hired for in-home viewing.

I wondered this about my deflowering.

Too few ever knew Saartjie Baartman, whose remains remained unburied for centuries.

———

Will these words be my offering? My body? My bread?

Is this an act of communion?

Pray for the blasphemous.

———

It's time to reel a man in. Black is ideal, but whoever will have her works.

—MORGAN JERKINS

———

The ponds in which I learned to fish, most swimmers were translucent.

———

*I learned that awareness mattered a lot more
to me than race.*

—MINDA HONEY

———

I tell myself something similar.

But do I believe me?

———

*Marriage rates are declining for black women
across the educational spectrum.*

—RICHARD V. REEVES and
KATHERINE GUYOT

———

According to the Pew Research Center, we are
also among the least likely to intermarry.

———

A family full of law enforcement, I grew up
and wanted to be a poet.

———

My mother taught me "Lift Every Voice and Sing"; double Dutch; and about Juneteenth. She taught me how to cut and cook collards, ribbons bathing in ham-hock water.

But for most of my twenties, I felt shame about my spades-related deficiencies.

———

I was twenty-three, and you were twenty-seven.

All of this forematter a part of what brought us together.

———

In the fifties, Richard Loving and Mildred Jeter were convicted of illegally marrying.

———

Their love was not an act of defiance.

—JEFF NICHOLS

———

But was mine?

———

If this were a memoir, it might start: "The fact that we loved each other was the hardest part."

The "we" being my family.

The "we" being you and me.

———

My favorite narrative arcs are the ones where lovers don't end up together: he boards a train; she stumbles into the street; they part after she loses a baby.

After imbibing these, it's hard to leave the trapped heat of my sheets.

———

In 2016, I bought tickets to the Virginia premiere of *Loving*.

I'd lived in Charlottesville for two weeks.

After buying the tickets, I learned Richard died a few years after the court case, then I finished rereading *Bluets*.

―――

Field research is primarily characterized by qualitative research though it may have quantitative dimensions.

―――

Frederick Douglass married Helen.

Alice Walker married Melvyn.

Jack Johnson married Irene, Lucille, Etta.

Serena Williams said she never thought she'd marry a white man.

I wonder if some of my Black poetry foremothers thought something similar.

―――

At a friend's housewarming, I lean into liquor
with a half dozen other Black women my age.

I don't know most of them, so they don't know
about you when they talk about wanting to
try out a white man.

We dissect white men like a breed—talk about
penis size and question their engorged flesh's
cotton-candy coloring.

———

Note: Of the penises I've seen, I haven't known
a Ken-doll mold made special for certain
coloring.

———

After someone submits that white people
smell like wet dog, I mention you, me.

Tell them for most of my twenties, I thought,
with you, I'd have offspring.

———

Minda Honey decided awareness is more
important than race.

I've decided I care less about size and more about if he knows what to do with it.

In the spirit of transparency, I'll admit that I am not at all indifferent.

———

The dissection moves from physical to emotional to being able to come home and talk about *those white people*.

I offer to the group: *then, why aren't we all with Black women?*

———

Defense mechanism: an unconscious psychological process intended to avoid conflict or anxiety.

———

Black Card Revoked™

———

On this I feel I need to be explicit: I do not covet whiteness.

34.

But what did loving you say about me, about tumorous tendrils of white supremacy?

———

In *Loving*, an attorney asks Richard, *What would you like me to say to the Supreme Court . . . ?*

Tell them I love my wife, he retorts.

———

Sometimes love is enough.

———

My mom was a chemist, so I've learned to say shit just for the reaction, learned the importance of the quantitative:

> I've been with ten men—six Black, four white.

But remember I'm not good at math, that not all of these are facts.

———

I'll admit this part not a fiction: only three men would say I've been their girlfriend.

All of them white.

All of them went on to make commitments to white women.

———

YOU can count on one finger the number of black men who can rightfully say they have been your boyfriend.

—SHAYLA LAWSON

———

I can count none.

———

To be clear, I didn't just fall for white boys.

I fell for Andrew and Andrew and Aaron, Richard and Rob, and other Black men with names too distinct to put them on blast here.

———

When I repeat the title of Damon Young's "Straight Black Men Are the White People of Black People" to a white friend, it breaks his brain.

I repeat it over and over again over the course of a weekend.

―――――

No one asks why Black men haven't dated me.

I'm asking myself the same damn thing.

Keep asking: what's wrong with me? Was it the pond-like beginnings?

―――――

I wish my life was less binary—1s and 0s amounting to nothing.

In the spirit of transparency, I'd love to never explain again my scarf, edges, or kitchen.

―――――

I think my mother used to worry I wanted to be white—one of three Black girls in my grade.

I didn't.

I just wanted to fit in—akin to most middle schoolers' sentiments.

———

I wanted to be Aaliyah.

Grieved for her the way white girls in the sixties mourned Monroe.

Raised in the era of Destiny's Child, Blaque, and 702, TLC and 3LW, I wanted to be a part of a Black girl group.

But I owned more Backstreet than B2K, though Boyz II Men and *NSYNC were both in heavy rotation.

I am still quick to go to Deborah Cox's "We Can't Be Friends" when, of you, I think of calling.

———

During those years when my mother had her fears, I did wish I had a "more complicated" backstory.

———

Regular black. The kind of black that . . . is over.

—TRESSIE McMILLAN COTTOM

———

In retrospect, I can explain the liminality with which middle-school me was grappling.

———

During an icebreaker for a multicultural program, there was that step-in / step-out community-building exercise.

You know, step in if you were ever picked on.

Step out if you've ever picked on someone else.

All in a circle:

Step out if you're African-American.

Step out if you're Black.

Two people remained.

Immediately targeted was the woman we read as Black for not identifying the way the group liked.

———

People say mixed kids are the cutest.

(See notes on "people.")

———

In the beginning of the *Dark Girls* documentary, a girl child doesn't want to be considered Black.

———

I call my niece *my brown sugar cube*—an explicit celebration of her rich pigmentation.

———

If I have a daughter, will she still be stuck in the Doll Test?

———

Accepting an award, Lupita Nyong'o explained that, as a child, she prayed God would lighten her skin.

———

I had begun to enjoy the seduction of inadequacy.

—LUPITA NYONG'O

———

I wish this was the only thing about which I was worried.

———

Black girls are missing; their disappearances rarely make TV.

———

I am also terrified of having Black sons.

How some white people don't know who Emmett Till was, I still cannot fathom.

———

Did you and I ever talk about him? About Trayvon Martin?

———

We discussed race like scholarship.

You occasionally thought aloud about it, about how you never wondered what it would be like to raise Black children.

———

Race was a linchpin on the periphery of our discussions—waiting for me to find it, me.

———

On that August day in Charlottesville, I was writing on an island in another state with a Black woman who turned twenty-eight.

Sandra Bland's eternal age.

———

the body: a home for love focuses on Black women's healing and self-love, about our survival of trauma.

———

Our sufferings do not magically end; instead, we are able to wisely, alchemically, recycle them.

—BELL HOOKS

———

Note: This is the plant.

Nothing virginal comes of this.

———

Someone once told me how her mother made a turtle of her melted wedding ring to signify how home is in the body.

———

What if I'm made of shell?

What if I go inside and cannot find myself?

———

What will these references be when I'm leathery? When I cease to be?

———

Note: I'm made anxious when rhyme feels easy.

———

Here, I'd like to record an observation: in your field study of 2011, I am probably the villain.

———

I knew nothing of *Loving* when we were together.

———

I often don't tell people the beginning of our ending.

You found photos of my former lover—a Black man a curled comma in my bed.

———

I never told you much about him, about the man I loved who never called me his girlfriend.

44.

He liked being little spoon, his six feet two wrapped in my five feet five cocoon.

I'd trace the Arabic tattooed on his chest, the name of his father on his bicep—map all the places he wouldn't let me.

But maybe I wasn't searching.

He would kiss the scar on my left breast, the nape of my neck, only told me he loved me when he knew we had nothing left.

———

With you, I told myself things would be different.

I'm slow to trust and, with you, I told myself I'd be someone new.

———

How could I tell you all of this when, like Ham's curse, for those photos, I worried I'd always be reaching for my purse.

———

Retributive love born of betrayal can be doled out across generations.

———

I never wanted to be indebted.

———

In a different crowded Thai restaurant in the center of a different state, a white man stepped behind the bar and served himself a beer, scoffed at the waitress's admonishment.

At a table next to him, a Black woman and I, for menus, wait for twenty minutes.

———

Perhaps, in Thai restaurants, men don't know how to behave.

Perhaps, I should stop living in the centers of states.

———

I guess it might begin with two men: one Black, one white.

———

At the winery where I worked, there were close talkers and white people who touched me without my permission.

There: my body was a novel treasure to white strangers with wined entitlement.

There: a white woman grabbed my face, said I looked like Corinne Bailey Rae.

There: an old white man asked me my favorite book. Knowing he wanted *The Bluest Eye*, *The Fire Next Time*, I said *The Great Gatsby*.

———

They were careless people, Tom and Daisy— they smashed up things and creatures and then retreated back into their money or their vast carelessness or whatever it was that kept them together, and let other people clean up the mess they had made.

—F. SCOTT FITZGERALD

———

A white woman after reading *Citizen*: *I finally get it.*

The "it" being me.

———

There: only a heightened state of here.

A daily existence.

Nothing micro about the aggressiveness.

———

With you, I was seven hundred and thirty-three shards of smashed glass, how many times we had sex according to my math.

But really, we were both trying to mosaic—drawing blood on each other's sharp edges.

———

Let's lose the glass imagery.

I was fresh scab I kept letting you pick—translucent layer before crusting.

When you left me, I took to finding my own openings.

———

After a breast biopsy, I removed the pressure bandages too early—my skin still pursed from this decision a decade later.

I was told I should've massaged the wound to break down scar tissue.

This is me rubbing.

———

Or am I a grief monster splicing sutures, bloodletting to regulate my humors?

———

I cannot breathe when a roller coaster is free-falling.

Everyone else screams.

———

Desire is a complicated thing.

In the Disney version, Pocahontas sings about how it's impossible to return to the exact same place, how nothing remains the same.

In reality, she didn't fall for Smith. She went with Rolfe, converted to Christianity, became Rebecca—wife of Isaac, the unsacrificed.

———

You cannot step twice into the same stream.

All entities move and nothing remains still.

—HERACLITUS

———

Still, I want the water of our first bath together—baptismal font in which I hoped to be reborn into someone who felt worthy of love.

I met you two months after he told me he no longer wanted to be with me.

———

In Disney, Pocahontas quotes philosophy.

In reality, Rolfe touted her as his civilized savage.

She died a year later.

———

For me, all the men who came closest to savagery were "civilized" men in a "universal" sense.

(At this point, readers should know what that *universal* meant.)

———

When the field was a field, where would I have been in it?

———

In Colonial Williamsburg, in front of a four-poster bed, a white woman asked me, *do you wonder what it would have been like to sleep on it?*

———

I never wanted to write about slavery or its legacy, but I cannot seem to escape the intergenerational reality.

———

Maybe one day I'll feel more Felrath Hines–free, writing *Radiant* on linen, loosed from this particular type of examination.

———

I rewatch *Mad Men* in winter, to try to recreate a river, replay "The Night We Met" and the entirety of the *White Lighter* album ad nauseam.

I like knowing where I'm going.

Maybe that's why I keep writing the same poem about how I fear the dawn—that blue-hue hour before sun we filled with talk of the babies that would never come.

After the 2016 election, "Total Praise" and "You Are the Living Word" were added to the rotation.

———

Note: Why am I writing this?

Note: Why do I write anything?

———

Lord Huron talks about love like a haunting.

———

Routine makes it easier to breathe when I want for the ache of ambering leaves.

I am relieved when the clock undulates at 4:44—the time at which my mother was born.

———

After you left, I stated proudly that you weren't the best thing to happen to me.

But still, you, I found myself chasing.

This a learned behavior.

Defense mechanism for not wanting to admit I felt the trace-paper-thin of leaf decomposition.

Typhoon's "Post Script" made a mantra of not loving unconditionally.

———

You said you did, that I didn't afford you the same courtesy.

We both constructed narratives in which I was not worthy.

———

Terence Nance's *An Oversimplification of Her Beauty* is not an interracial love story, but a white man took me to see it, said *for us it was metacommentary*.

In the film, a Black man falls in love with a Black woman who stood him up for a date, and he makes a film about it.

I tried to parse how, for us, this was meta.

Years later, I still wonder where my date's girlfriend thought he was when he spent the night complimenting my complexion.

Now, Nance has an HBO show.

That white guy didn't end up marrying that particular white girl.

―――――

We are constantly guarding our words and actions for fear of a live autopsy.

—AIRA JACKSON-SAMS

―――――

To be clear, in 2010, I know I was a villain, had sex with more than one man who had a girlfriend.

―――――

In these notes, I'd like to resist any myth about Black women as monolith.

We are a complex calculus for which the limit does not exist.

(Kudos if you think this a *Mean Girls* reference.)

―――――

We do not have to become a mix of indistinguishable particles resembling a vat of homogenized chocolate milk.

—AUDRE LORDE

———

I hope we build a body politic so thick with contradictions and nuance and humanity and blackness (because blackness is humanity) . . .

—TRESSIE McMILLAN COTTOM

———

I could tell you I was going through something, but it's important for me to be allowed to be a flawed human being.

———

Note: This is an investigation of the effects of the world on one woman's desire and identity formation.

That mouthful more digestible than the parameters of our failure.

This, to me, more clearly metacommentary, as is admitting that writing these things brings me anxiety.

———

Here I am razor-ripped, asking for forgiveness.

But not from you.

Who?

Me?

———

These things that happened before we met are the fillets I flayed, laid bare on a platter for you on our first date.

I wanted to get to the meat, the medium-rare center, the pink.

I understand, then, when you said, *I don't think I'm a good investment of your emotions*, you might have meant, *I don't think you are a good investment of mine.*

———

You once tried to trap me in a lie, asked if I thought it was acceptable to keep a stash of photos of a former lover.

Not at all, I replied. Kept on about my life.

———

We both knew me to be a terrible liar, always teeming with eager glee.

I get this from my father—notorious for telling me what gift he's gifting.

It's strange, his inability to do this when he's so secretive about other things—skill sourced from top secret clearance in the military.

This, too, a learned behavior, a lesson.

———

You thought you no longer knew me. The ease with which I lied.

The reality: I had no idea.

Forgot the box in which the photos were hiding.

––––––

When I lied to you, we both know.

The mis-sent *I still love you* text.

It was meant for him.

––––––

Oh, the perils of love in the digital age.

––––––

This was a year before the photos.

Perhaps we were always ending.

––––––

When you were building your case for me
being untrustworthy, you never submitted
this as evidentiary support, but I knew it was
in the discovery.

––––––

Cue "The District Sleeps Alone Tonight" by
the Postal Service.   59.

But why didn't I listen?

Why your words am I so willing to manipulate to make me out to be the villain?

———

I don't think I'm a good investment of your emotions.

—YOU

———

A premonition and a promise.

———

Too many married men have told me I'm the one that got away.

Too many single men have told me I'm not the kind of girl you just date.

Either way, I've been single for half a decade.

———

Audibly, I muse: *will I ever have sex again?*

———

You liked to say you didn't cheat because you had already broken up with me, even though we found ourselves interlocked question marks each morning.

———

The men I have loved have always lied to avoid confrontation or take responsibility for inappropriate behavior.

—BELL HOOKS

———

We stayed together because it was too hard to be apart in a metro area of 6.2 million.

———

How much of want is need?

How much of fear is why I've been single for five years?

In our culture, privacy is often confused with secrecy.

—BELL HOOKS

A therapist once called me a soothsayer—not in the fortune-telling way but from the Old English for *sooth* meaning *truth*.

I let her believe I didn't have my own capacity for secrecy.

Note: What is truth in poetry?

What exists in the gaps?

The only sin she's committed is being familiar.

—JOAN HARRIS

Well, not really.

But still, you fucked a *sticky redhead.*

Note: Your words, not mine.

———

Between 2016 and 2011, you told me you loved three other women.

Throughout it all, I was there for blue-hue-hour phone calls.

———

I hope she knows you only like the beginnings of things.

—FAYE MILLER

———

This doesn't include the at least three women you slipped into over those years: one white, one Black, one Panamanian.

———

Note: I recognize the problematic nature of limiting people to race and countries of origin.

They are documented here the way, to me, they were presented.

———

I do not know white people's points of origin.

I'll admit, most of my life, this hasn't felt important.

Do they care from what country I come? So why about white people's histories should I be certain?

What does this erasure say of me? Perhaps revealing an envy that I can't chart my course further than plantations without DNA testing.

———

Importance is subjective.

It's good to have comprehensive observations.

———

I think you once said your people were British.

———

You thought you might have gotten the Black woman pregnant.

There's also the woman about whom you're uncertain—your memories of the night divergent.

———

For many of these, you made known, they happened while you were in the memory-free zone.

———

A different white man I thought I could know called the memory-free zone *going to Narnia.*

———

You traveled to that space more than anyone I've known, commended yourself when you hadn't visited in a month.

———

My memory makes nets from twines never meant to be knotted.

I kept finding myself drawn to the glimmering silk of your web.

—————

We were toxic, tasty, the spicy-food shits of our twenties.

We were hot wings and buffalo mac & cheese; vindaloo and chili; the "whore's nachos" with Hormel, Tapatío, and cheese, jalapeños perhaps the only green.

—————

She's stringing you along, but she's not committing to you, but she's keeping you around, just in case, like an old can of chili in the pantry.

—ROBIN SCHERBATSKY

—————

In this you are "she," but I know how you felt about chili.

One of the women with which you fell in love had money but ended up stealing your identity.

Her, you told me, you thought you could marry.

Was this your version of exposure therapy?

———

Once I asked if you'd stay with me, if I treated you poorly.

———

I'd like to inject that old refrain: *hurt people hurt people.*

We were both hurting.

———

Not many dishes from my childhood have survived.

The heat-resistant stoneware fissured from time.

I don't remember there being whole sets—
only begin to grapple with this when I start
considering having my own children.

———

Three months before we stopped speaking,
I met a gentle man who sang Sinatra, had a
warm laugh.

He read a different book in which I tried
to write about you—asked if there was a
violence.

———

Your parents disapproved of the slap bet we
had.

Scolded like children, we never played in
public again.

———

I didn't know then he was writing about men's
hands on women.

———

I hate to admit I was afraid you'd leave.

This is the way I never wanted to love anybody.

———

A different therapist asked me to evaluate my
learned behaviors.

———

The first time I was near climax with a man, I
couldn't stop crying.

I remember the knuckled knobs of his penis,
how wet for weeks I was from wanting.

I'm still ashamed by this because he wasn't a
man I wanted to want me.

This was 2010.

He was a white man.

———

Do white men compliment the Wonder Bread
complexion of the white women they bed?

———

Perhaps I'm afraid to be seen.

———

I want . . . painful, difficult, devastating, life-changing, extraordinary love.

—OLIVIA POPE

———

That's how I've been trained.

———

It's not just *Scandal*.

It's *Archer*, *The Words*, and *How to Get Away with Murder*.

———

Pop culture taught me that with sex, I should say *no* before I say *yes*, that the best love will induce Pavlov salivation.

———

What is the nature of consent?

I don't remember saying *no*.

Know I didn't say *yes*.

———

My body, oft a site of confusion: a lingual love,
but not intestinal, for gluten; my cholesterol's
craving for fiber it cannot compute.

———

Every day that I exist I acknowledge that
being alive is an act of resistance.

———

I can't figure out the line between love and
want, need and desire.

But it's fishing-line thin, made of polyethylene
fiber.

———

In our field, we grew "avocados" into our safe
word when we played an *Eternal Sunshine*   71.

of the Spotless Mind–type pillow smother game.

———

Note: Is this an act of erasure?

———

One time, pillow-mouthed, my elongated *av-o-ca-do* resembled *oh, god, help me.*

You didn't stop, said it wasn't the safe word, admonished me.

I remember this story ending with us laughing.

———

When the field was our bed, I found myself quieted—wanting to be whomever to which you'd be most attracted.

———

We see movies in which people are represented as being in love who never talk with one another, who fall into bed without ever discussing their bodies, their sexual needs, their likes and dislikes.

—BELL HOOKS

———

It wasn't likc that with the Black man before you. He asked what I wanted, fulfilled my greatest physical needs like a five-course meal of delicacies.

After, I'd fondle his ear crease as he snored into the deep.

We'd both wake in wanting.

Unable to articulate our truest selves, our morning sex would be tight-lipped.

———

It wasn't like that with you either—your hand slipped between my legs while you whispered me a bedtime story.

———

Note: I never knew what either of you wanted, am still figuring out where to put my limbs.

———

Once, after we weren't together, someone who loves you told me that I deserved someone better.

———

If I'd ever really been together with him, I wonder if our story would've had a place to begin.

———

After you, I carried on a brief dalliance with a white man working abroad with refugees.

He was someone with whom I'd gone to college.

He pined for me secretly, admitted he could only confess this because he was in another country.

———

Confession: an admission of guilt, shame, or embarrassment.

In religion, an admission of sin in hopes of absolution.

———

Fuck *Loving v. Virginia*, antimiscegenation still on Alabama's books until the turn of this century.

(And still, and *still*, Black women tried to save it.)

———

In 2019, eight states, to marry, required a declaration of race—one of which was the one in which I went to college.

So for him—yes—*confess*.

When he returned stateside, he started seeing a white woman, said he'd still like to fuck me.

He's not one of the men for which I fashioned myself home-wrecker.

———

You know what that is?

It's growth.

—KELLI

———

Media sold me a fucked beauty standard and a belief that problematic love becomes happily ever after.

But it's not just through pop culture I learned the link between love and decimation.

———

After the *Loving* premiere, all I wanted to do was to take a bath with you.

We spent years in tubs too small for us— triangled knees and elbows trying to prop us up.

———

I was raised by a kind of love that was so inextricable from pain . . .

—CATHY PARK HONG

In my Charlottesville apartment, I finally had a tub big enough, but I knew there was no recovering an *us*, so I stood outside in the rain hoping you were standing under a similar mist in your mountains.

A few days later, I'd learn you were living with a woman.

———

What color is she?

—BETHANY BISME-LYONS

———

Because even when we aren't talking about race we are.

It's inextricable from how I exist in this world.

———

Oceans could separate us, but no matter where we stand in them we're touching.

Can the same be said of the night sky?

———

I've always sought the pole furthest from the one I know.

———

In Australia, I was lost under the Southern Cross.

———

The reality: I've never lived more than a few hours from home.

———

I worry that being nobody's happily ever after makes me nobody.

To be nobody is to be no body is to be weightless.

I could use more levity.

I worry that not being anyone's happily ever after makes me no one, which could also mean I'm never alone.

———

In my adult life, I've loved two men—one Black, one white.

For most of my twenties, they both remained in orbit.

You are one of them.

———

You have to be twice, my mother said.

You have to be twice, Papa Pope said on *Scandal*, bestowing the same adage.

If I'd had a baby at twenty-three, I would have told it the same thing.

(See: ballet story.)

———

To forget a wound and scratch it issues a special kind of pain—the pain of the wound and the pain of having to acknowledge it's no longer forgotten.

The second sometimes hurts more than the first.

———

My brother's first fiancée is no longer with us.

———

It's easier to move forward knowing that something, anything, if not the river, will stay the same, like a song looped, though only in the digital age.

A scratch in the rimmed memory of a record will render a new permanent forever.

———

Sometimes I remember this when I hold my nephew's face to kiss, when my niece bares all her teeth in the midst of giggling.

———

Unaccustomed to affirming attention, living in rural centrals and places that bloom red in elections, I am skittish at compliments, shy

around the Black guy who smiles repeatedly
as we both browse bookstore aisles.

———

Twenty-three-year-old me lived in her body.

———

Note: I returned to our city to write portions
of this.

Everything has shifted down to the positioning
of things in galleries.

Woman Eating (1971), once a main display, is
now in a corner, tucked away.

We didn't know this world of wireless
headphones, the strong, public skunk of
marijuana.

———

About us, the first poem I wrote: "Pot Smoke
and Glasses on the Casio."

But it was really about the first white guy I
loved.

(See, there's a breakdown in my mathematical systems.)

How he needed me like I needed to know I belonged anywhere, to anyone.

_____

The twenty-three in me is a whisper.

_____

After you, I went on a few dates with a straight-edge vegetarian—a medium-build, pillow-lipped Black man.

_____

Note: I swing hard when I swing to the land of opposites.

_____

He wanted a *good woman, one who would listen.*

_____

Because of a lack of respect elsewhere, the men in these scenarios value a measure of subservience and submission from women that is intended to make up for what they can't receive in the wider world.

—MIKKI KENDALL

———

My mom was young mother turned bread-winner turned boat owner.

I know nothing of subservience, submission.

———

The vegetarian said he had nothing but respect but frequently did not come correct.

I once stopped him in the middle of a sentence, made the following declaration:

> *my mom gets buck*
> *my brother carries a gun*
> *and my dad loves me more than*
>   *oxygen.*

———

After you, I learned better how I belong to them.

———

The twenty-three in me is a shout.

———

I remember telling you you were worth good things.

From you, I think women before me stole something.

———

Sometimes I can't remember if it's gravel or graphite lodged in my palm, but I know I was wounded, forever altered.

———

I don't know where the rupture began.

———

I don't think it's ironic that *whole* has a *hole* in it.

———

It's hard for me to admit that from me I think
you stole something.

———

What is the distance between dream and
nightmare? Between there and terror?

An imperceptible fissure in a tank.

———

The new forever: the two men I loved are both
fathers to daughters and sons.

Me: mother to no one.

Me: mother to dead ovum.

———

Some nights, waves howl at a hidden moon—
the sky a cloak of clouds and heat lightning
lighting the ominous.

Some nights, mosquitoes feast on me—leaving
welts on my newly sunned skin.   85.

Tonight, I'm the kind of ripe where I realize you're at my fingertips—the ones that traced sun-raw tan lines, wound coils in your thicket.

Perhaps it's because, tonight, I am ovulating.

———

Is the Colosseum beautiful because it's destroyed or because it's still standing?

———

For what was my body a vessel?

For what will it be?

———

Note: I am preoccupied with mothering.

———

I could have had you. I could have shamed you into being with me. But I didn't.

—PEGGY OLSON

———

I couldn't; you wouldn't.

I wanted other things.

———

The new world was built on the ruins of what had been unmade, destroyed.

—DIRK WIEMANN

———

If it weren't for ruins, I wouldn't be writing.

———

I suppose it is possible that one day we will meet again and it will feel as if nothing ever happened between us.

—MAGGIE NELSON

———

The first time we saw each other after a year, there was a hunger in our hands—a want, a need.

———

Someone who loves me told me no one gave a fuck whether I lived or died when I was a teen.

———

I needed him to see me to make myself feel worthy. And now look at us—two dark-skinned sisters playing out the same story, giving everything over to a man who sees us in a world that doesn't.

—ANNALISE KEATING

———

I know someone terrified to turn corners, of what might happen—splash of hot coffee, tip of a knife.

I tease her for this.

———

We haven't spoken in over four years, and I still bring you up at parties.

This turns my stomach like the stench of a
kale-wrenched bowel movement.

———

*Minds can become Frankensteins, and you've
gotten gun-shy of yours and the noises it
makes in the night.*

—NELL BOESCHENSTEIN

———

My aunt watched loops of murder-mystery
marathons while tumors masticated her.

The illusion of knowing where things were
going.

The story goes: someone is murdered, and
someone pays the price.

Or doesn't.

———

Netflix: *are you still watching?*

As daunting a question as *are you dating?*   89.

———

I've told myself that thirty-five is the ideal age
to have a child.

———

Once upon a time, I thought I'd been found.

———

Ada Limón teaches a craft class on duende
and the ladder, about going into the darkness
and climbing out.

———

Fuck Eve's curse, I'd be grateful for the chance
to give birth.

———

Twice as many Black women as white ones die
from childbirth-related complications.

———

It wouldn't be the first time, for want or need,
90.   I made a choice that might hurt me.

———

Could being alive be my ladder?

———

The duende-ladder poet shares she knows a woman who doesn't drink tea because the choice is between tepid or scalding, between limbo and hell—what we choose when we drink tea, which I consume almost exclusively.

———

Note: This is a larger life commentary.

———

Is it the Taurus in me seeking the path of most resistance: single parenthood, poetry, and, once upon a time, you?

———

I love the title of Barbara Guest's *The Location of Things*—such simplicity.

Placing stick-stars at random in my teens, I unintentionally ordered them diagonally.

―――

I believe in rhyme and reason, in a season's final scene.

I want to believe that I can be whole with a hole in me.

―――

In conversation with two Black women, we wonder whether it's even worth dating— their marriages streams of smoke after the explosion of a firework.

We discuss hair texture and nipple color; wonder why we don't feel fuckable.

(See: Lupita Nyong'o; see: Damon Young.)

―――

No matter how many books I read, no matter how many degrees, these realities make me sicker than anything.

―――

When the field's a marital bed, most of the non-Black women of color I know share theirs with white men.

———

Confirmation bias: the tendency to see that which confirms what you might already believe.

(See: Douglass; Walker; poetry foremothers.)

Small data sets yield inconclusive evidence.

———

You went to an HBCU.

I went to a predominately white institute.

(See: ponds in which I learned to fish.)

———

In college, your counterpart in my binaric history of paramours I made myself a fool for.

I risked ruining other relationships for a glimmer of him, still find something tectonic-shifting about this man who never named me as his girlfriend, still swoon at his *happy birthday, love* texts.

———

Did he know my middle name?

How I got that scar?

Would he remember the make and model of my first car?

I'd ask the same of you, but I already know the truth. You could barely remember I was born in May, let alone which day.

———

Perhaps, my father is right.

I don't want to be seen.

———

This isn't a swan song for him because, like you, I will always love him, because even though he and I had different beliefs about thunder, we both have an abiding faith in rain.

———

One friend asks: *would you ever marry a white man?*

Another thinks I've said: *I don't date Black men.*

Like a game of telephone, there's a breakdown in the language.

———

In jest, a Black girlfriend and I joke about what it's like dating white men.

How did my furniture get here?

When did we adopt a cat?

———

In reality, four months in, you asked me what color rings I'd consider wearing.

———

I'm . . . realizing just how important it is in our world—and in the overwhelmingly

white spaces that we move within—to be
unapologetically in love with our blackness.

—NAILAH CUMMINGS

———

Narrative maps the geography of me, of
becoming.

I'm not Beyoncé; I didn't wake up like this.

It has taken three decades, but I'm beginning
to plot my course confidently in the abyss.

———

This country meant for us to be small, and
the most radical thing that we can do is to
choose to be our whole selves.

—REV. ANGEL KYODO WILLIAMS

———

My brother told me the story of Jacob's hip—
swagger sourced from brokenness.

———

When you are free, you lead with your weakness.

—JERMEIR JACKSON STROUD

———

I don't know what I believe, but these biblical stories live in me.

———

The idea isn't to remove the blemish but to move forward with a beauty mark.

—JERMEIR JACKSON STROUD

———

I am beautiful.

I am complete.

I love the twenty-three in me, down to my pigeon-toed feet.

———

But I didn't then.

Was your love a reflection?

———

In *Runaway Bride*, Maggie Carpenter tries to find her signature egg style.

When my parents split, I told my mom this.

Since she doesn't eat any of the sort, the analogy falls short.

I was trying to welcome her to my cohort.

———

I worry pop culture puddles me but even more about all the white shit I'm referencing.

———

It's easier to share my sexual proclivities in poetry than to allow myself to be seen.

Easier to be naked under a sheet, a masseuse finding knots in need of kneading.

———

After you left, I barely saw myself.

This a deprivation.

——————

But what if someone doesn't love the me I let them see?

——————

7. Tell a Black person in your life you love them just because they exist.

—*HARRIET'S APOTHECARY*

——————

I have to tell myself.

It's important.

——————

In my early twenties, I worked on an epistolary series.

I didn't know I wrote a book-length suicide note.

I titled it *And If I Die Before I Wake*.

A prayer and a promise.

———

I'm alive; I'm alive; I'm alive.

Cry it with me.

It doesn't always feel like it, but it's a good thing.

———

We don't talk about mental health enough in the Black community.

———

In the midst of all this, my love for you feels as though it requires a reckoning.

———

This field feels like I'm being hunted.

———

You told me I was 90% perfect, but there was 10% you couldn't work with.

Note: The twenty-three me was bad at math.

My me-now math figures I'm a mother-fucking goddess.

———

How much did race play into your calculations?

———

128. Take a deep breath to honor your Black life.

129. Take an even deeper breath to honor your Black life.

—HARRIET'S APOTHECARY

———

Walking hand in hand to the free tax clinic, you stopped and pivoted when a Black man grabbed himself, asked if I wanted to know what it's like to be with a real man.

Here: you arrived at the penis size.

My dear cunnilingus connoisseur, in this there was no reason for you to feel inferior.

———

Fetish: a devotion or worship of something for its assumed magical powers.

———

You were the first person, other than me, to bring me to climax.

———

When the field's a bed, I note the flush of a white man's neck as he approaches climax, the way he moves like someone who has something to prove.

It's like those years I only fucked younger men.

———

The ways I gave myself to you.

The ways I didn't.

———

Let's be honest, I've fudged some of this math.

It can't start with two men: one white, one Black.

There were three men, still only one with any pigmentation.

I'm not sure about which I'm more concerned: the fact that I'm zero for three or the imbalance of this weighting.

———

Note: I'm learning not to fall for just anyone who wants me.

———

I almost did this with the pillow-lipped vegetarian.

He told me, if we had kids and couldn't agree about parenting strategies, he'd be the tiebreaker—rooted it in godliness, in a holy covenant.

From him, I was able to walk away.

First from *Oversimplification*, then from Refugee Relief, then from this man for whom I needed more piety.

———

From you, I think I gained something.

———

As a teen, I wanted to design clothing.

I forget about this until, when I am an adult, a pipe burst in my childhood home.

The house: outside—sturdy, nothing more; inside—stripped down to the subfloor.

———

This was the beginning of my parents' divorce.

Well, one of them.

Like us, their end had many beginnings.

———

Among the papers I dried, a sketch of midriff-free dress, in an "Are You That Somebody?" Aaliyah-style.

On it I note the textiles.

Back then, I didn't know I didn't know things.

All the fabrics synthetic.

I didn't have enough cloth to touch to know from which I'd like to construct.

———

I didn't have a lot of patterns for a healthy relationship, so I ran myself raw constructing as an act of negation.

———

Together we read: *How to Be an Adult in Relationships*.

———

When you asked what color bands I wanted to wear, we were on our way home from my brother's wedding.

When we landed, you found out you might be becoming a parent, asked me if I'd consider raising the baby together.

———

Note: I ask two writers on a panel about "the stories of mixed-race Americans struggling to break free of Black and white stereotypes" about how, in their work, they grapple with interracial desire.

We discuss the research—the dearth—my fear of what might be unearthed.

———

In *Light Girls*, Dr. Allyson Hobbs discusses how white men raped enslaved black women, how this violence is "part of what produced a lighter-skinned population."

———

I never wanted to write about slavery but here
it is, again.

It has always been.

Will it always be?

———

I pass no paper bag or comb test.

Was I a disappointment to my great-gran?

———

According to my mother's 23andMe or her
results on Ancestry, she's 80% West African.

We don't talk about the Scandinavian.

We don't talk about these things like the man
I didn't really want inside of me.

How I fucked one again and again in an act of
reclamation.

How I see it now as an attempt at negation.

—————

Somewhere, someone's breaking.

—————

Am I attracted to things that will break me—
moth drawn to flame, paper wings incendiary?

—————

Am I product of intergenerational love and
survival?

—————

Somewhere, someone is persisting.

—————

I'm not going to say all of the right things.

I want to, but, again, I'm merely just me.

—————

I cry every time Erik Killmonger dies—from
the world took everything away from me all
the way through his final plea.

When a white woman tells me she can't teach with a migraine, I think of how I lecture for my ancestors.

For better or worse, fragility is not a narrative in which I am well versed.

Sadly, the real truth, which is a taboo to speak, is that this is a culture that does not love black [men].

—BELL HOOKS

To be clear, I love Killmonger, have loved Killmonger, will always love him.

It might be easy for Mike Kelley to piss all over this since canonical literature reflects his version of the human condition.

We cannot and will not abandon our sons, brothers, fathers, husbands, or friends, because for us they do not represent the enemy.

—MIKKI KENDALL

———

This is not a failing of Black men.

This is a fracture in the system.

———

I want Killmonger to be reincarnated as N'Jadaka—the man we (I) can love with less tension.

———

Admitting I want a man challenges my independent underpinnings.

But maybe this want is something different entirely.

———

In *The Incredible Jessica James*, there is not much conversation about the races of the leading lovers: Black woman and white man.

Critics said that this was out of character for the eponymous leading lady.

Some critics criticize early episodes of *Scandal* for this.

While I agree, I'm grateful you can be skin-to-skin with someone pigmented differently and for that not be the conversation only.

———

This may seem radical for the predominantly white filmmakers who work in this genre, but it's important to remember that black girls' lives aren't solely defined by racism.

—ANGELICA JADE BASTIÉN

———

I learned you were having a child while I feared a mass on my ovary.

On a bath mat at the foot of that Charlottesville tub, I cried until my teeth hurt.

It was not lost on me, the irony, that my body was positioned fetally.

I didn't know you were already writing letters to your child's mother the last time we were together—your palm against my left breast, warm breath on my neck.

In retrospect, I'm quick to make the puzzle pieces fit.

How that type of touch was your limit.

———

What if I'm irreparable?

———

A squirrel darts, skitters into the street.

We are not the only creatures who live in a state of anxiety.

———

Note: This is the felling of haunted wood.

———

Our last week together, you took me to a church: Episcopalian. Everyone processed to receive communion.

I crossed my arms against my chest—didn't take the sacrament.

———

The reality: race was infrequently on the periphery for you and me.

———

There were many clues that meant you didn't know what it meant to be me.

Your lamentation at how I would cross the street if a man was following too closely.

How, when you were driving, you never took note of the types of flags that were flying.

———

None of the people in the pews at the church looked like anyone who was taught to fear the world since birth.

———

You thought walking street-side and sitting door-facing was what I needed in terms of protecting.

And still, and still, I loved *you* anyway.

———

You opened the door to your house in the city in which we both lived.

The first time you saw me I didn't know it was our beginning.

———

With white women, I stalked through a small-town dark alley.

Mounting a porch, one said: *is this it?*

I announced, backpedaling, *I'm too Black for this shit.*

—

On your front steps, your reaction I read as displeasure.

Later you'd tell me, you were trying not to stare.

—

So much lost; so much gained; so much need from verbal communication.

—

The door was glass and oak—floor-length mirror the first pane between us.

—

At twenty-three, my clothes were thigh-baring.

—

After six months, I let you take me on a catamaran into the Caribbean—transparent the depth as the shoreline lurched away.

I sat quietly, confident you knew not what you were doing.

———

Too many Black women die silently suffering.

Is this the fate of our progeny?

———

Why America's Black Mothers and Babies Are in a Life-or-Death Crisis

The answer to the disparity in death rates has everything to do with the lived experience of being a black woman in America.

—LINDA VILLAROSA

———

Thankfully, this hasn't been my story.

Not yet.

———

Me: mother to dermoid with skin, hair, and toothlike structure as opposed to cancer blossom.

I'm still sore from the remembering, the forgetting, the remnants of Frankenstein stitches monstering my belly button.

———

My dad the first person I called.

He knew when he answered the phone that something with me was wrong.

He said he could tell from the way I said *hello*.

Only one other person has been able to do this that I've known.

———

Admitting this fucks up my argument.

———

It is easier to articulate the pain of love's absence than to describe its presence and meaning in our lives.

—BELL HOOKS

———

You were, are, a human being.

To me, that really means something.

———

You won't recognize yourself in this crude effigy.

I, too, prefer to remember us through rosé-filled glasses in the pink dusk of a mid-Atlantic summer.

But you were Natty Lite by day. By night, a Rouge IPA.

I have to admit, I don't miss the stale of a secondhand-beer kiss, the way hops leaked from your pores in morning.

———

The first night we kissed. I'd burned my leg on the exhaust pipe of your Kawasaki.

You warned me about the heat.

Repeatedly.

———

To you, apparently, I was never listening.

———

You sat me on the edge of my couch, used vinegar to pull the heat out.

I first felt your lips pressed to the flesh of my right knee.

———

It felt good to be desired by you, by the other white men whose desire had been packaged for me on television.

———

Note: In the contract for this, I promise not to write anything materially inaccurate.

I tell my agent this a fiction.

Can you tell what I've changed to protect you?

Me?

What I've altered for the sake of poetry?

———

You would be proud of me for writing.

You'd be proud of me.

You'd be proud.

———

A baby lives in your old home.

The Walgreens up the street is empty, gutted.

I wish I would have stayed longer in your neighborhood, observed the porch better—it was smaller than I remembered.

I wish I would have asked to climb those back steps, the ones on which, when it rained, pots sat; gone into that bathroom—a late add, floor atop earth—seen if it was ice in the bowl instead of toilet water.

But I was still Black in a white neighborhood, so down the street I strode appreciating the spit of rain and the click of my heeled boot.

On our first date, too, I wore impractical shoes.

———

I still pray for you, your family—the old and the new.

———

Note: People who know me would find this prayer odd.

Note: People who know me wouldn't find it odd at all.

———

Baduizm taught me about intellects.

It was early I learned the layers of code-switch.

———

Another note on God: I have no idea what I believe and what is residual, but I know I'm prone to fall to my knees.

I hear nothing from above, but I wonder how it all began, where my energy goes when my body decomposes.

———

I am told the Big Bang may have never happened.

I am told the universe is ever expanding.

———

But where was I, I asked when I was young about the years that predated my existence, unsatisfied with the answer that I had not been born yet.

———

I like to make meaning of things.

Right eye twitch: good is coming.

Rain: my aunt is with me.

The red, wrinkled necks of dead baby birds on my doorstep: something's about to end.

In addition to *How to Be an Adult in Relationships*, we read *My Utmost for His Highest*—a daily devotional—and *Extremely Loud & Incredibly Close.*

Our respective pages delineated by handmade bookmarks labeled "His" and "Hers."

———

A man named Ángel is gentle with me when about you I start writing.

A woman named Angèle asked me if I love myself.

———

It's hard to purge yourself of someone in the digital age—a mix of deletions, filters, and blocking agents.

The paper is the hardest to part with: the Valentine's Day card you made—the back with your name and age proudly displayed.

The "New Kids on the Block" ornament constructed with Popsicle sticks featuring a photo of you and my six-month-old nephew.

It was hard to make them garbage.

———

The first time we fucked, our sex-wet skin clung.

Like packing tape, you could hear us come undone.

———

The first time you used the word *love*, you arrived at my door at dawn, scalp caked in your own blood.

Said it wasn't the only time you'd come to me like this.

Told me I didn't have to feel the same with a kiss.

———

When people show you who they are, believe them.

—MAYA ANGELOU

———

I waited until the next blue-hue dawn to use my own articulation of love.

———

It begins with Chaos.

Eros follows.

———

You drew out *baby*, so it became portmanteau: inset preceded by body of water.

———

The term would become a pacifier for 6 a.m. phone calls: *bay-bee* I'm fine, *bay-bee* I'm hurt, *bay-bee* I want to come home.

After one, I took photos of your battered body for a police report: scalp to occipital bone, rib

125.

cage, scapula, boysenberry blossoms all over
your torso.

———

The first rule about fight club . . .

—CHUCK PALAHNIUK

———

Did I journal when we were together?

I can't remember.

———

I was ensnared in the hive of our love.

———

As a college writing adjunct, I taught *Fight
Club* to discuss subculture.

———

Nature taught me to be tantalized by that
which I can't understand—the complicated
126. thatch of a sturdy bird's nest, the way water

can carve a canyon—that which cannot be tamed.

———

Cartographer, you were the mountains from which you come. I—the ocean.

I know, like me, you were desperate to map yourself in something, someone.

———

The second rule about fight club . . .

—CHUCK PALAHNIUK

———

Some of the characters here are untrustworthy.

———

Ford Strong, you believed in God and gun and country.

Your pecs pressed into my blades, trying to absorb the shock of my recoil as we took aim.

———

Once you subluxated my rib, told me to relax
as you pushed it back in.

We were playing "Pin the Shoulders," which
would join the slap bet and pillow play in
games that no longer took place.

———

On our first date, you took me into the
woods, told me land navigation was your
specialization.

Note: For a brief moment I wondered if only
straight white men killed women this way.

Down an embankment, my sandals slipped
on a rock, and in your arms I found myself
caught.

As I steadied myself, our fingertips feathered
each other's.

We'd recount to our friends that we held
hands that day.

———

You were a man I held drunk and weeping.

You were a man who said to your girlfriend, I meant nothing.

———

You are like windblown sand, silt still in my crevasses.

———

I am corkscrew wrenched.

Even though you're gone, I still feel the hollow you left.

———

Years later, the woman from the basement of the church turned place of poetry worship told me she doesn't want you to be my whole romantic history.

———

I once punched you with a closed fist.

For that, I am, and will always be, sorry.

You were cruel to me, then heartbroken when
you thought that hit had ended things.

———

Once, when you were memory-free, you
mushed my face while calling me *bay-bee*.

Against my chest, you apologized, you wept.

———

I don't know why with myself I am so terse
while forgiveness for you is so well rehearsed.

———

Yes; I watched *Scandal* until its end, until, to
me, it no longer made sense.

*You're intrigued by the representation of
interracial desire*, the Black woman said.

That was 2015; I still feel haunted.

———

Some languages may have many words for snow, but what's the word for loving each other despite ourselves?

What is the word for weeping when I knew it was the last time I'd know your body—your canvas mapped in tattoos and scars?

———

The tenderest game we played: the caress of each other's anatomy with words that began with *b*.

———

In view of a mountain you climbed, I cried at the sight of a sunbathing lady and her baby.

———

Belly.

———

Once, I craved a cookie, savored the taste until it was mushed mash and spit, baby-birded the muck into your mouth.

You swallowed it.

———

Beard.

———

You said you grew one when you were feeling
not quite like yourself, told me as I scratched
your scruff.

You wore one the entire second year of us.

———

Back.

———

I used to trace the vertebrae of your shortened
spine—injury to your back deeper than you'd
ever let me.

There are no words for the wick worn thin
between us.

Hiraeth the closest.

———

Brows.

———

Before the blue-hued morn after that blood-dried night, I knew how I fclt, kncw from the moment on the porch where I listened to you play "Make You Feel My Love" in an early June rainstorm.

You used the edge of your nail to scratch the brown bend above your hazels.

This before that first kiss.

———

Breast.

———

A buoyant body caught in the undertow gets pulled into the swell.

The waves continue to come.

Ceaselessly.

———

Bare.

———

We wanted to have a family big enough to play the Feud.

———

We polled one hundred people and asked them how they feel about their exes.

Answer: Grateful for the time we had together.

Answer: I wish we'd only ever been friends.

Number one answer: I wish I'd never met them.

———

I still don't regret that we met.

———

It begins and begins and begins.

134.

It begins with you, with me—it begins with me growing up a Black girl in a predominately white world in the nineties.

———

Tsunamis recede, leaving debris—crumpled car, slanted echo of a housing structure— from pressure under which only sea monsters can exist: fangtooth, angler, vampire squid.

———

I thought I was the ocean.

———

My father is one of the people that, from my voice on the phone, immediately could tell when something was wrong.

You were the other one.

———

This can be beautiful fact, but both of your actions still have long-lasting impacts.

———

One of you spiderwebbed a windshield with your fist, the other dead-eyed and cold when you're pissed.

———

For romantic love, I have few role models.

Just people in need, hoping in someone else to find something.

———

But I don't want any man to be my beginning.

———

I am not of Adam, not Eve.

I am atom of a cataclysmic event, of matrilineal makings.

———

It starts with the egg of me inside my grandmother.

It starts with my future follicles inside my mother.

———

Maybe it begins with a generational curse I'm manhandling and trying to burst.

———

Don't write about what you're not willing to cannibalize.

—SHARA McCALLUM

———

Within these wombs, we've learned the strength to part with part of ourselves.

———

I don't want to be Hagar in my car weathering the weight of expulsion.

Don't want to await a fate, then have to disguise myself like Tamar.

That's why I'm in the field; that's why I'm studying.

———

I still don't know things.

———

Is this a poem, a prose, a prayer?

———

I'm a mess of genres—for which there are no nouns of assembly.

———

In *Field Study Part Two: The Redo*, I have brown-skin twins, with hair twice as thick, and laughs as rich as chocolate.

In this future tense, it might only be me and them.

———

Even as I accrue these notes, I'm still not sure I've found the pulse.

———

I can barely taste the pale of persimmon,
feel palmed powdered snow, do not know the

sound of someone else hiccuping inside my hollow.

———

I'll rewrite a history only to have a copyeditor write it again. The designer will render the whole thing a palimpsest, palindromed because I am both all and none of it.

It the singular; *it* the collective. A collective use of nouns of assembly:

      an ambush   a bale   a bed

          a herd   a murder

I worry this is an unkindness.

———

No matter how far I go, there is never enough makeup for the bullet hole.

That's the middle *i* in *reviver*; the story I don't tell that returns.

———

I'm just one woman working toward resolution.

———

The reality: I loved "Ex-Factor" before you ever met me.

———

For better or worse, words so unlike the river.

———

We only spent two years in repose together in eagle pose, a few short spikes on an EKG monitor—the frenzy of tachycardia.

———

I've taken part in many a guided, purge-related ritual: sage smoke and palo santo.

We weren't something to be burned, buried, or flushed like piss, shit, or blood.

We, for me, were something worth examining.

———

When I returned to our city, I visited my old haunts—what a strange word to describe a place once loved.

———

Since you, I've lived no place longer than a year or two.

———

What does it mean to feel I belong to nowhere?

To be constantly creating new sites of ruin?

———

The city sounded the same: the clinch and cinch of a bike's gearshift, the honk of a bus running a red.

There was a chorus—discordant, a symphony of syncopation, though this was not "The Entertainer."

———

Perhaps I treat new places like new loves.

Perhaps I, too, only like the beginnings.

———

I'm desperate for a headboard but cannot commit.

———

Am I a tourist to my own existence?

———

For fear of choosing poorly, I choose nothing.

Again and again.

———

See, you and me are not the only thing for which I have an overanalytical capacity.

———

Perhaps I still haven't mastered the 5 A's of how to be an adult in a relationship: attention, acceptance, appreciation, affection, allowing.

———

The most important relationship is the one with yourself.

This "you" here is me—not anyone else.

———

The last time I thought we might be a pair, I was twenty-seven. We fought in an orderly Restoration Hardware.

I said, *I want a life that fits this*—living room staged with gray couch and oblong accent ottoman.

You told me you didn't want any of it— fingering the ribbed stitch of a throw's fabric.

———

Can we call a spade a spade?

A game neither of us had yet played.

———

Codependence: emotional or psychological reliance on someone, especially if one person

suffers from an illness or addiction or
depression.

———

Enter: me as witness to the slow removal of
sutures on the raw wounds of marriages.

———

In an act of rejection, I went ahead and
replicated something different.

———

The last time we spoke, you wanted to know
the name of the place with the sweet potato
waffle fries piled high with BBQ duck and
bacon.

———

I want to believe that there was never a
question of whether there was sun, but that
because of where we were it just eclipsed us.

———

Two weeks later, I'd learn you were selling your furniture, moving to be with her.

This was less than a year after Restoration, just a year before you welcomed a baby.

―――――

What you meant was you didn't want me.

―――――

I miss your hair ensnared between my fingers, the deep breath of your runner's lungs, the way you used to rub together your pointer and thumb.

―――――

When I wonder if I'll ever have sex again, I mean I wonder if someone will love me.

If I'll let them.

If I'll let me.

―――――

Probably not this methodically, but I do wonder if you think of me.

———

I hope you find whole with all the holes you see.

———

Love takes courage, and I no longer think myself brave.

Or, maybe, it's that I'm braver than I've ever been.

———

I hope you never read this.

I hope you do.

In the failing light of summer, I'm forgiving me. I've cannibalized you.

Additional Data

in order of appearance

epigraph from Tressie McMillan Cottom's "Girl G," in *Thick: And Other Essays* (New York: The New Press, 2019).

Reference to Cheryl D. Hicks's "'Bright and Good Looking Colored Girl': Black Women's Sexuality and 'Harmful Intimacy' in Early-Twentieth-Century New York," in *Journal of the History of Sexuality* 18, no. 3 (September 2009).

Reference to Shonda Rhimes's *Scandal* (2012–2018).

from Mike Kelley's "Hollywood Filmic Language, Stuttered: *Caltiki The Immortal Monster* and *Rose Hobart*," in *Foul Perfection: Essays and Criticism*, ed. John C. Welchman (Cambridge, MA: MIT Press, 2003).

from a tweet by Lupita Nyong'o (November 9, 2017).

Reference to Kenneth B. Clark and Mamie P. Clark's "Emotional Factors in Racial Identification and Preference in Negro Children," in *The Journal of Negro Education* 19, no. 3 (1950).

from Damon Young's "Living While Black Is an Extreme Sport," in *What Doesn't Kill You Makes You Blacker: A Memoir in Essays* (New York: Ecco, 2019).

Reference to Toni Morrison's *The Bluest Eye* (New York: Holt, Rinehart and Winston, Inc., 1970).

Reference to John Musker and Ron Clements's *Aladdin* (1992).

Reference to Christopher Nolan's *Inception* (2010).

from Ross Gay's "An American Drama: Fictional Representations of Black/White Interracial Desire from 1894–2001," Temple University, ProQuest Dissertations Publishing, 2006.

from Zora Neal Hurston's "How it Feels to Be Colored Me," originally published in *The World Tomorrow* (1928).

Reference to Hagar in the Book of Genesis.

from Tressie McMillan Cottom's "Black Girlhood, Interrupted," in *Thick: And Other Essays* (New York: The New Press, 2019).

from Damon Young's "Straight Black Men Are the White People of Black People," *The Root*, September 19, 2017.

from bell hooks's *We Real Cool: Black Men and Masculinity* (New York: Routledge, 2004).

from Claudia Rankine and Beth Loffreda's *The Racial Imaginary: Writers on Race in the Life of the Mind* (Albany, NY: Fence Books, 2015).

from Morgan Jerkins's "The Stranger at the Carnival," in *This Will Be My Undoing: Living at the Intersection of Black, Female, and Feminist in (White) America* (New York: Harper Perennial, 2018).

Reference to *Hall v. DeCuir* (1877).

Reference to *Plessy v. Ferguson* (1896).

from Kiese Laymon's *Heavy: An American Memoir* (New York: Scribner, 2018).

from "#44. Loving, Living, Learning: A Liberated Life Talk with Rev. angel Kyodo williams," *Black Girl in Om* (podcast), June 25, 2019.

Reference to Evelyn Brooks Higginbotham's discussion of respectability politics in *Righteous Discontent: The Women's Movement in the Black Baptist Church, 1880–1920* (Cambridge, MA: Harvard University Press, 1993).

from Audre Lorde's "Uses of Anger: Women Responding to Racism," in *The Master's Tools Will Never Dismantle the Master's House* (London: Penguin Modern, 2017).

Reference to 2017 United States Senate special election in Alabama.

from Joss Whedon's *The Avengers* (2012).

from Cheryl D. Hicks's "'Bright and Good Looking Colored Girl': Black Women's Sexuality and 'Harmful Intimacy' in Early-Twentieth-Century New York," in *Journal of the History of Sexuality* 18, no. 3 (September 2009).

from Jay Karas's *Ali Wong: Baby Cobra* (2016).

from Natasha Trethewey's "Taxonomy," in *Thrall* (New York: Mariner Books, 2015).

from Morgan Jerkins's "How to Be Docile," in *This Will Be My Undoing: Living at the Intersection of Black, Female, and Feminist in (White) America* (New York: Harper Perennial, 2018).

from Minda Honey's "The Reality of Dating All Men When You're Black," *Gawker*, June 24, 2014.

from Richard V. Reeves and Katherine Guyot's "Black Women Are Earning More College Degrees, but That Alone Won't Close Race Gaps," Brookings Institute, December, 4, 2017.

from Gretchen Livingston and Anna Brown's "Intermarriage in the U.S. 50 Years After Loving v. Virginia," Pew Research Center, May 18, 2017.

Reference to J. Rosamond Johnson and James Weldon Johnson's "Lift Every Voice and Sing" (1905).

Reference to *Loving v. Virginia* (1967).

from Jeff Nichols, quoted in Andrea Mandell's "Exclusive: These 'Loving' Re-Creations Will Move You," *USA Today*, November 1, 2016.

Reference to Jeff Nichols's *Loving* (2016).

Reference to Maggie Nelson's *Bluets* (Seattle, WA: Wave Books, 2009).

from Shayla Lawson's "Intraracial Dating," in *This Is Major: Notes on Diana Ross, Dark Girls, and Being Dope* (New York: Harper Perennial, 2020).

Reference to Deborah Cox's "We Can't Be Friends (ft. RL)," *One Wish* (1998).

from Tressie McMillan Cottom's "Black Is Over (Or, Special Black)," in *Thick: And Other Essays* (New York: The New Press, 2019).

Reference to D. Channsin Berry and Bill Duke's *Dark Girls* (2011).

from Lupita Nyong'o's speech delivered at the *Essence* Black Women in Hollywood Luncheon (2014).

Reference to the website for the body: a home for love, a nonprofit organization focused on helping Black women heal from sexual trauma.

from bell hooks's *All About Love: New Visions* (New York: HarperCollins, 2001).

Reference to Ham's curse in the Book of Genesis.

Reference to Toni Morrison's *The Bluest Eye* (New York: Holt, Rinehart and Winston, Inc., 1970).

Reference to James Baldwin's *The Fire Next Time* (New York: Dial Press, 1963).

from F. Scott Fitzgerald's *The Great Gatsby* (New York: Scribner, 1925).

Reference to Claudia Rankine's *Citizen: An American Lyric* (Minneapolis, MN: Graywolf Press, 2014).

Reference to Eric Goldberg and Mike Gabriel's *Pocahontas* (1995).

Reference to Rebecca and Isaac from the Book of Genesis.

from Heraclitus, as quoted in Plato's *Cratylus*.

Reference to Felrath Hines's *Radiant* (1983).

Reference to Matthew Weiner's *Mad Men* (2007–2015).

Reference to Lord Huron's "The Night We Met," *Strange Trails* (2015).

Reference to Typhoon's *White Lighter* (2013).

Reference to Richard Smallwood's "Total Praise," *Praise and Worship* (1990).

Reference to Fred Hammond & Radical for Christ's "You Are the Living Word," *Purpose by Design* (2000).

Reference to Typhoon's "Post Script," *White Lighter* (2013).

Reference to Terence Nance's *An Oversimplification of Her Beauty* (2012).

from a conversation with Aira Jackson-Sams.

Reference to Mark Waters's *Mean Girls* (2004).

from Audre Lorde's "Learning from the 1960s," in *The Master's Tools Will Never Dismantle the Master's House* (London: Penguin Modern, 2017).

from Tressie McMillan Cottom's "Thick," in *Thick: And Other Essays* (New York: The New Press, 2019).

Reference to the Postal Service's "The District Sleeps Alone Tonight," *Give Up* (2003).

from bell hooks's *All About Love: New Visions* (New York: HarperCollins, 2001).

from "Christmas Waltz," Matthew Weiner's *Mad Men* (season 5, episode 10).

from "Tomorrowland," Matthew Weiner's *Mad Men* (season 4, episode 13).

from "Hooked," Craig Thomas and Carter Bays's *How I Met Your Mother* (season 5, episode 16).

from "Nobody Likes Babies," Shonda Rhimes's *Scandal* (season 2, episode 13).

Reference to Adam Reed's *Archer* (2009–).

Reference to Brian Klugman and Lee Sternthal's *The Words* (2012).

Reference to Shonda Rhimes's *How to Get Away with Murder* (2014–2020).

Reference to Ivan Pavlov's classical conditioning experiments.

Reference to Charlie Kaufman and Michel Gondry's *Eternal Sunshine of the Spotless Mind* (2004).

from bell hooks's *All About Love: New Visions* (New York: HarperCollins, 2001)

from "Hella Questions," Issa Rae's *Insecure* (season 2, episode 2).

from Cathy Park Hong's "Bad English," in *Minor Feelings: An Asian American Reckoning* (New York: One World, 2020).

from Russell T. Davies's *Years and Years* (episode 4).

from "It's Handled," Shonda Rhimes's *Scandal* (season 3, episode 1).

Reference to Duane Hanson's *Woman Eating* (1971).

from Mikki Kendall's "It's Raining Patriarchy," in *Hood Feminism: Notes from the Women That a Movement Forgot* (New York: Viking, 2020).

from "Meditations in an Emergency," Matthew Weiner's *Mad Men* (season 2, episode 13).

from lecture by Dirk Wiemann.

from Maggie Nelson's *Bluets* (Seattle, WA: Wave Books, 2009).

from "Vivian's Here," Shonda Rhimes's *How to Get Away with Murder* (season 6, episode 2).

from Nell Boeschenstein's "Now That Books Mean Nothing," *The Morning News*, December 8, 2011.

Reference to Ada Limón's lecture on craft, "On Duende & the Ladder: Mystery and Hope in Poetry," June 12, 2018.

Reference to Barbara Guest's *The Location of Things* (New York: Tibor De Nagy, 1960).

from a conversation with Nailah Cummings.

from "#44. Loving, Living, Learning: A Liberated Life Talk with Rev. angel Kyodo williams," *Black Girl in Om* (podcast), June 25, 2019.

Reference to Jacob in the Book of Genesis.

from a conversation with Jermeir Jackson Stroud.

Reference to Garry Marshall's *Runaway Bride* (1999).

from "365 Days of Affirming Black Life and Amplifying Black Love," *Harriet's Apothecary*.

Reference to the music video for Aaliyah's "Are You That Somebody?," *Dr. Dolittle: The Album* (1998).

Reference to David Richo's *How to Be an Adult in Relationships: The Five Keys to Mindful Loving* (Boston: Shambhala Publications, 2002).

from Bill Duke's *Light Girls* (2015).

Reference to Ryan Coogler's *Black Panther* (2018).

from bell hooks's *We Real Cool: Black Men and Masculinity* (New York: Routledge, 2004).

from Mikki Kendall's "Solidarity Is Still for White Women," in *Hood Feminism: Notes from the Women That a Movement Forgot* (New York: Viking, 2020).

Reference to James C. Strouse's *The Incredible Jessica James* (2017).

from Angelica Jade Bastién's "Why Do Teen Dramas Like *Riverdale* Keep Sidelining Black Female Characters?," *Vulture*, May 10, 2017.

from Linda Villarosa's "Why America's Black Mothers and Babies Are in a Life-or-Death Crisis," *The New York Times*, April 11, 2018.

from bell hooks's *All About Love: New Visions* (New York: HarperCollins, 2001).

Reference to Erykah Badu's "On & On," *Baduizm* (1997).

Reference to Oswald Chambers's *My Utmost for His Highest* (New York: Dodd, Mead & Co, 1924).

Reference to Jonathan Safran Foer's *Extremely Loud and Incredibly Close* (New York: Houghton Mifflin Harcourt, 2005).

Reference to Maya Angelou in conversation with Oprah Winfrey.

from Chuck Palahniuk's *Fight Club* (New York: W.W. Norton & Company, 1996).

Reference to Bob Dylan's "Make You Feel My Love," *Time Out of Mind* (1997).

from a conversation with Shara McCallum.

Reference to Tamar in the Book of Genesis.

Reference to Lauryn Hill's "Ex-Factor," *The Miseducation of Lauryn Hill* (1998).

Reference to Scott Joplin's "The Entertainer" (1902).

Reference to David Richo's *How to Be an Adult in Relationships: The Five Keys to Mindful Loving* (Boston: Shambhala Publications, 2002).

Acknowledgments

Anyone who has been along for this journey knows that there were many times that I wanted to stop writing—fearful of the form and wary of letting people travel with me through my mind palace. I know all writers say they couldn't have done this without their communities, but I truly mean it when I say thank you to everyone who made the existence of *Field Study* possible.

First, I must thank Shara McCallum and Ángel García, who both asked critical questions of me in 2016, which led me to this book. Your generous, kind, and inquisitive spirits have helped me arrive here.

Thank you to my editorial team and everyone at Farrar, Straus and Giroux and FSG Originals. Thank you to Jonathan Galassi, for taking an interest in my voice despite me not yet knowing where this project was going, and to Jackson Howard, for your patient editorial style that gave me time to explore. I so appreciate the way you knew when I needed big-picture feedback and when I needed you to get into the weeds with me. And a special thanks to Jennifer Baker, for your thoughtful and precise eyes, your difficult questions, and your advice on restorative practices, as I finished this book in the midst of great stress and uncertainty.

Thank you to Kerry Sparks, my agent, for jumping in with both feet when this book was in its infancy and for continuing to cheer me on through frustrations and doubts; imposter syndrome is real. And, of course, I am ever grateful to my collaborator and literary sister, Shayla Lawson, for connecting me with Kerry but also, importantly, for your love.

A big thank-you to the Hedgebrook Writers in Residence program on Whidbey Island, where I first shifted *Field Study* from a short essay to a prose poem. And I cannot thank my Hedgebrook sister Deborah Harkness enough for giving me the opportunity to return to Whidbey in 2019. It was in your house, Deb, that I figured out the arc of this project—the failing light of summer peeking through the windows. And I cannot talk about Whidbey without talking about Dantiel W. Moniz—whom I met at Hedgebrook in 2017 and who returned to Whidbey with me—for introducing me to oysters, rewatching *Mad*

Men, and being unwaveringly confident in my capacity to complete this book. You talked me down and lifted me up. Thank you. As strange as it may seem, I'd also like to thank Whidbey Island—a place that provided me with the spark I needed.

Field Study would also not have been possible without the support of a grant from the Delaware Division of the Arts—a state agency, in partnership with the National Endowment for the Arts—and the support I received from the College of Arts and Sciences at Bucknell University. Thank you to all my colleagues who continued to encourage me to carve out time for my work.

I also want to thank all of the Black women who have held space for me while I was writing *Field Study*, especially Alexandria Brown, who showed me strength and asked for *more*; Nailah Cummings, who has given me more love than I often feel I deserve; Jaila Ingram-DeBerry, who encouraged me to take care of myself; and Aira Jackson-Sams, who laughed, thought, and vented with me. Each one of you holds such a special place in my heart.

And there are more people in my community than I can name, but I do want to extend special gratitude to María Alvarez, E. G. Asher,

Niya Bates, Sara Chuirazzi, Andrew Ciotola, Christian Coleman, Cymone Fourshey, K. A. Hays, Maisha Kelly, Angèle Kingué, Martha Park, Joe Scapellato, Kaya Washington, Shannon Woodloe, and Nikki Young for your love, kindness, and eyes. I would also be remiss if I didn't thank the ever talented and generous Diana Khoi Nguyen, whose care, encouragement, and craft continue to propel me; thank you for being so present in those fifteen-day bursts in which so much of this book was written.

As always, thank you to my family. Thank you to my parents, Chyrrea and Gordon Sebree, for encouraging me to use my voice, even when we all may be afraid of what I might say. I am grateful for the values you both instilled in me. Mom, you've taught me resilience; without you, I would not be the inquisitive, voracious reader I am. Dad, you've taught me generosity, and I am always working to see myself through your loving eyes. I love you both like the ache I feel for ambering leaves. And thank you to my brother, Jermeir Jackson Stroud, whose sage wisdom I can always turn to; Pop Pop would be proud. I also want to thank Crystal Stroud, as well as my niece and nephew, Jordan and Charli, for continuing to show me the ways love can manifest. Thank you all for being my squad, for seeing me when I don't want to be seen, for encouraging me to see myself as whole despite all the holes I see.